Al Qaeda and the Global War on Terror

A Monograph
by
Major David R. Waters
United States Army

EMENS EST CLAVIS VICTORIAE

School of Advanced Military Studies
United States Army Command and General Staff College
Fort Leavenworth, Kansas

AY 2010

Abstract

AL QAEDA AND THE GLOBAL WAR ON TERROR by MAJOR David R. Waters, U.S. Army, 50 pages.

The United States is now in the eighth year of the Global War on Terror (GWOT). For America, the war began with the surprise attacks against targets in Washington D.C. and New York City on September 11, 2001. For al Qaeda, the war began centuries ago. Since the attacks of September 11th, the United States has failed to win a decisive strategic victory over al Qaeda. This monograph asks why. It contributes to the body of knowledge needed to understand the enemy and the operational environment of the Arab Muslim world, with the aim of increasing the effectiveness of America's future wartime efforts against global jihadist movements in general and al Qaeda in particular.

The monograph explores aspects of the Arab Muslim world which al Qaeda exploits and depends upon for their survival, and then examines al Qaeda itself. The research includes text, speeches, and analysis of Islamic thinkers such as Seyyed Qutb, and key jihadist leaders such as Osama bin Laden and Ayman al-Zawahiri.

While not the only threat to American national security, al Qaeda is the threat that has proven capable of conducting complex and horrific attacks on a global scale. Therefore, the United States and its allies must decisively defeat al Qaeda in order to dissuade the further expansion of the global jihadist movement.

Table of Contents

Introduction

America is at war with an elusive, adaptive, and ruthless enemy. It is an enemy unlike any faced in the past; one that eschews an identifiable uniform, has no state of its own, does not abide by Western rules of warfare, hides amongst civilian populations, can attack U.S. targets at home and abroad, cannot be deterred, and relies on the use of terrorism and propaganda to further its cause.[1] This enemy is al Qaeda, an organization that has emerged as the leader of a global jihadist movement.[2] It uses off-the-shelf technology, the interconnectedness of the increasingly globalized world, and the freedoms of the Western world and the grievances of the Middle Eastern world to advance a new social order based on a seventh century religious ideal.

Despite lacking a state from which to draw resources or raise an army, this committed group of religious zealots has been at war with the United States since the 1990s.[3] In that time, they destroyed two United States embassies, attacked, and nearly sank, a United States Navy warship, and inflicted the worst terrorist attack on American soil in U.S. history. In addition, they have survived nearly nine years of the Global War on Terror (GWOT) with the United States and

---

[1] Bruce Hoffman, *Inside Terrorism* (New York: Columbia University Press, 2006), 2-3, 16. According to Bruce Hoffman, a professor at Georgetown University's School of Foreign Service, terrorism is "planned and systematic violence – or, equally important, the threat of violence – used and directed in pursuit of, or in service of, a political aim committed by non-state actors." In other words, terrorism is a means to an end.

[2] Peter Bergen and Paul Cruickshank, "Is Al Qaida in Pieces?," *The Independent* (June 22, 2008), under "al Qaeda," http://www.independent.co.uk/news/world/asia/special-report-is-al-qaida-in-p.htmls-850606.html (accessed April 20, 2010). The authors reported that in the summer of 2000, bin Laden hosted a five-day strategy session of 200 jihadists from around the world, noting, "[t]he leaders of most of the jihadist groups in the Arab world were there and almost everybody in within al-Qa'ida." to discuss ". . . where they were going and the lessons of the last 20 years."

[3] Bruce Lawrence, ed., *Messages to the World: The Statements of Osama bin Laden* (New York: Verso, 2005), 23. In "A Declaration of Jihad against the Americans Occupying the Land of the Two Holy Sanctuaries," Osama bin Laden authorizes defensive jihad against the Americans for their continued presence in the Kingdom of Saudi Arabia in October, 1996. Bin Laden released a second declaration of war on February 23, 1998 with a call to "kill Americans everywhere." Osama bin Laden, "Declaration of the World Islamic Front for Jihad against the Jews and the Crusaders." *The NEFA Foundation*, http://www.nefafoundation.org/miscellaneous/ FeaturedDocs/nefaubfatwaworldislamicfront.pdf (accessed March 24, 2010).

its many allies.[4] Likewise, since September 11th, 2001, its members conducted, assisted, or inspired successful attacks throughout Europe, Africa, Asia, and the Middle East. Recently, they came within a breath of destroying a passenger jet over Detroit on Christmas Eve, 2009.[5] In many instances, al Qaeda maintained the initiative against its foes, adding to their appearance of strength and competence. This is a considerable feat considering the military and economic might of the United States and its allies in the late twentieth and early twenty-first centuries.

The central question at this time must be this: What has prevented the United States from decisively defeating al Qaeda? Why, after years of great effort and expense, is there still no end in sight?[6] As the Obama administration leads the United States into the next chapter of the GWOT, with a new surge of effort into Afghanistan, reassessing the strategic situation and the threat becomes crucially important. [7] The rationale behind this inquiry is simple: the failed efforts of the U.S. to capture bin Laden and defeat al Qaeda indicate an underestimation of the enemy and an incomplete understanding of the operational environment.

This monograph asserts that America cannot defeat an enemy it does not understand. Specifically, an incomplete understanding of the enemy and the operational environment is critically hampering the efforts of the United States and its allies in the GWOT. In light of this assertion, it explores and broadly examines the operational environment of al Qaeda and the Arab

---

[4] The term "Global War on Terror" (GWOT) is used throughout this monograph to avoid confusion between the various names used to refer to America's war against al Qaeda, such as "The Long War," or "Overseas Contingency Operations." GWOT is the most enduring and well-know name for the American military response to the 9/11 attacks.

[5] Eric Lipton, Eric Schmitt, and Mark Mazzetti, "Review of Jet Bomb Plot Shows More Missed Clues," *New York Times* (January 17, 2010), under "Terrorism," http://www.nytimes.com/ 2010/01/18/us/18intel html (accessed April 15, 2010).

[6] Amy Belasco, *Congressional Research Service Report for Congress: The Cost of Iraq, Afghanistan, and Other Global War on Terror Operations Since 9/11,* Congressional Budget Office, http://www.fas.org/sgp/crs/natsec/RL33110.pdf (September 28, 2009). According to the CBO's estimate, ". . . the GWOT could total [between] $1.3 trillion to . . . $1.8 trillion for FY2001-FY2019."

[7] While the Obama administration doubles down in Afghanistan, it also faces rising tensions over Iran's ambiguous nuclear program; a stalled Israeli-Palestinian peace process; and the tenuous situation in Iraq, including the unknown results of Iraq's 2010 elections, the effect of the scheduled U.S. troop drawdown, and Iraq's ability to govern without significant U.S. assistance.

Muslim world on which al Qaeda depends. With the intention of reassessing the enemy and its environment, the paper is motivated by the words of Sun-Tzu, who wisely called warfare "the greatest affair of the state, the bases of life and death, the Way (Tao) to survival or extinction. It must be thoroughly pondered and analyzed. . . . [t]he victorious army first realizes the conditions for victory, and then seeks to engage in battle. The vanquished army fights first, and then seeks victory."[8] Whether America is to be victorious or vanquished depends on its ability to realize the conditions for victory before engaging in the battle. Obviously, the GWOT cannot come to a full stop while military planners and policymakers reconvene to analyze the enemy. Yet it is important to take a step back and reevaluate, refocus, and learn. America cannot just "fight first…then seek victory."

This monograph explores the topic of America's war against al Qaeda. It strives to shed light on areas of understanding that planners potentially overlooked when the United States first designed its response to the 9/11 attacks, many of which continue to plague America's efforts to defeat al Qaeda today. Its purpose is to inform, not to argue in favor of one policy or another. After all, any proposed policy or strategy should spring from a fundamental understanding of the situation and the key players involved. This paper is a small step toward achieving that understating. The first section highlights key values, norms, and beliefs of the Arab culture with the intent of establishing a more complete understanding of the social factors that allow and in many ways enable the success of an insurgent movement such as al Qaeda's. Additionally, this section briefly discusses the historical development of the Muslim world's strained relationship with the West in general and the United States in particular. These social and historical factors feed al Qaeda's fire, motivating its members and in a sense making this insurgency less abhorrent to the Muslim world at large. The second section of the monograph shifts gears to focus directly on al Qaeda itself. After discussing the environment from which this Sunni Islamic insurgency

---

[8] Sun-Tzu, *The Art of War* (Boulder, CO: Westview Press, 1994), 167, 184.

emerged, it goes on to detail their goals, motivation, and logic. Finally, this section highlights the attributes that both help and hinder al Qaeda's existence within the Muslim world.

An understanding of the operational environment in which al Qaeda exists, including the values, norms and beliefs of the Muslim world and their historical interactions with the West, is important for several reasons. First, without a clear understanding of this complex environment, the United States' foreign policy in the Middle East and strategy against non-state actors such as al Qaeda will be reactive in nature or inefficient at best. At worst, it may actually strengthen the enemy or make the situation more complicated. As stated in the Army's counterinsurgency doctrine, FM 3-24, "[d]esigning operations that achieve the desired end state requires counterinsurgents to understand the culture and the problems they face."[9]

Next, understanding the environment is vital in any attempt to accomplish the three goals of defeating international terrorism outlined in the 2002 National Security Strategy, which include "to disrupt and destroy terrorist organizations of global reach; to strengthen the homeland against future attacks; [and] to wage a war of ideas to win the battle against international terrorism."[10] The West can only effectively wage this war of ideas if its representatives at all levels of government fully understand the broader meaning of the ideas at stake. Ideas such as spreading freedom and democracy may sound heroic and clearly worthwhile to American or European ears. However, as further discussed later in the paper, these same concepts may evoke a complicated and negative emotional reaction from foreign audiences, especially those with a history of exploitation by authoritarian regimes hiding behind the façade of democracy.

Unfortunately, America has a long way to go in the war of ideas. In the 2009 Arab Public Opinion Poll conducted by the Saban Center for Middle East Policy at Brookings, six Arab

---

[9] Department of the Army, *Field Manual 3-24: Counterinsurgency* (Washington, DC: Headquarters Department of the Army, December 2006), 1-28.

[10] George W. Bush, *The National Security Strategy of the United States of America* (Washington, D.C.: The White House, September 2002), 5-6.

nations indicated that nearly seventy percent of the respondents had a negative impression of America, and only twenty-two percent indicated that they had a positive impression.[11] While the United States is not and should not be in the popularity business, it is concerning that none of the nations polled had more than nine percent of respondents indicating a "very favorable" impression. In contrast, at least thirty-two percent of respondents in five of the six nations indicated a "very negative" impression. If the U.S. is to win the war of ideas and defeat al Qaeda and al Qaeda-like organizations, it must endeavor to understand the circumstances that fuel these negative perceptions. America's strategists need to identify the source of this distrust, hatred, and anger towards America. To do this, one must appreciate the unique values, norms and beliefs of Arab culture, their historical narrative, and the effect that propaganda and Islamic theories have had in shaping the perceptions and beliefs of the Arab people.[12]

The two parts of this monograph, the first focusing on the environment and the second on the enemy, complement each other and take steps to better inform the reader of the problem the West has had in defeating al Qaeda. They reveal al Qaeda's dependence on the passive and active support of the Arab Muslim world, and their ability to tap into the widely-held grievances of that world to propagate their own version of the truth. In this version of reality, the Muslim world gains hope, pride, and a sense of returned honor through al Qaeda's stance against the West. In Robin Hood-like fashion, Osama bin Laden embodies competence, leadership, and selfless service in a part of the world relatively devoid of such leaders.

---

[11] Zogby International, *Arab Opinions on President Obama's First 100 Days: A 6 Nation Survey* (May 2004), http://www.aaiusa.org/page/polls/6%20NationPPT%20Finl.pdf (accessed April 4, 2010). The nations surveyed were Egypt, Jordan, Saudi Arabia, Lebanon, Morocco, and The United Arab Emirates (UAE). When asked, "Generally speaking, [what] is your attitude of the United States," the UAE had the most favorable responses with 52% indicating a positive attitude and 40% a negative one. Egypt had the most negative opinion of America with only 14 % indicating a positive attitude and 78% a negative one.

[12] Clearly, much of the information used for the research of this monograph was not available or widely known during the design of the original strategy to defeat al Qaeda. Therefore, critiquing or placing blame is not the intent. Instead, the objective is to further the knowledge needed to defeat al Qaeda, warn of the continued threat from al Qaeda, and help guide potential strategy against al Qaeda-like organizations in the future.

The Poisoned Well: Understanding
Al Qaeda's Permissive Environment

To conceptualize accurately the scope and inherent challenges of the GWOT, one must understand how this enemy, as a quintessential yet unparalleled insurgency, operates within its environment. At its most fundamental level, al Qaeda's organization, goals, and tactics fit the U.S. military's definition of an insurgency, in that it is ". . . an organized movement aimed at the overthrow of a constituted government through the use of subversion and armed conflict."[13] The U.S. Army's *Counterinsurgency* manual lends more specificity to the definition, clarifying that, ". . . an insurgency is an organized, protracted, politico-military struggle designed to weaken the control and legitimacy of an established government, occupying power, or other political authority while increasing insurgent control."[14] Al Qaeda differs from this concept of insurgency in that its agenda goes beyond the borders of single state ambitions. Instead, they pursue global lines of effort with regionally focused goals against any nation not governed my sharia law.

Accepting that al Qaeda is an insurgency, the first section of this monograph describes the Arab Muslim world's environment within which al Qaeda lives and draws the bulk of their resources, security, and legitimacy.[15] This is an important concept to understand while conceptualizing the GWOT, because as the U.S. Army's counterinsurgency (COIN) doctrine states, "[A]t its core, COIN is a struggle for the population's support."[16] This identifies one of the

---

[13] Department of Defense, *Joint Publication 1-02: Department of Defense Dictionary of Military and Associated Terms* (April 12, 2001), http://www.bits.de/NRANEU/others/jp-doctrine/jp1_02(01).pdf 214 (accessed March 15, 2010).

[14] Department of the Army, *Field Manual 3-24: Counterinsurgency* (Washington, DC: Headquarters Department of the Army, December 2006), 1-1.

[15] David Galula, *Counterinsurgency Warfare: Theory and Practice* (St. Petersburg, FL: Hailer Publishing, 2005), 136. In the closing remarks section of his book, Galula closed by advising counterinsurgents to "[b]uild (or rebuild) a political machine from the population upward. All insurgencies rely on the population for support." The battle between the insurgent and counterinsurgent is over the population.

[16] Department of the Army, *Field Manual 3-24: Counterinsurgency* (Washington, DC: Headquarters Department of the Army, December 2006), 1-28.

central challenges America faces in the war: fighting a regional insurgency who understands the operational environment, customs, traditions, values, and narrative better than America can ever hope to. After all, al Qaeda is the so-called "home team." This means that American planners, policymakers, and leaders must endeavor to learn as much as possible in order to level the playing field.

Values, Norms and Beliefs of Arab Culture

With only six tenths of a percent of Americans claiming to be Muslims and relatively low levels of immigration until well into the twentieth century, many Americans have long remained ignorant of the Muslim world and the Middle East.[17] The ideological distance between these two cultures has existed for centuries. Bernard Lewis, a professor of Islamic history at Princeton University and noted expert on the Middle East observed, "[u]ntil the eighteenth century, the world of Islam had been cut off from almost all intellectual and cultural contact with the West. The Ottoman Empire in the days of its greatness maintained no resident embassies abroad."[18] Not until World War II would the two cultures, American and Middle Eastern, began to interact. Furthermore, it arguably took decades before average Americans paid attention to Middle Eastern or Islamic issues, culture, or current events. Yet, to compete with al Qaeda and al Qaeda-like organizations, the West must understand Arab values, norms, and beliefs, along with the common perceptions Arabs have of the West.

Two quintessential Arab values that merit scrutiny include the notions of honor and blame. In *The Arab Mind*, a seminal work on Arab culture, professor Raphael Patai explains that Arabs tend to cherish personal honor and pride above all else, and that they tend to blame others,

---

[17] Central Intelligence Agency, *World Fact Book,* http://www.cia.gov/library/publications/the-world-factbook/geos/us.html (accessed April 10, 2010).

[18] Bernard Lewis. *The Middle East and the West* (New York: Harper Torchbooks, 1966), 37-38.

even Allah, for their failures and shortcomings.[19] In a society that cherishes pride and honor above all else, their position in the world must be a hard pill to swallow. Bernard Lewis concurs, suggesting that "following is bad enough; limping in the rear is far worse." He goes on to assert that "[b]y all standards of the modern world – economic development, literacy, scientific achievement – Muslim civilization, once a mighty enterprise, has fallen low."[20] Section two of this paper illustrates how groups like al Qaeda, who pledge to restore Arab pride and honor, exploit this situation.

With or without predatory groups like al Qaeda, the Arab tendency to blame others creates a potentially dysfunctional environment in which they do not address the source of the problems because they mislabel the cause. One does not have to search long to find examples. Imam Sayyid al-Sharif, AKA Dr. Fadl, one of the original members of al Qaeda's top counsel, and the only member with legitimate Islamic credentials, writes, "The Palestinian cause has, for some time, been a grape leaf used by the bankrupt leaders to cover their own faults."[21] In an article posted on the website Jihad Watch, an Iranian by the name of Amil Imani claims that the frequent and distasteful practice of "ascribing blame to others and legitimizing their victimization" has regrettably "become a way of life with the rabid Islamists. As [distasteful] as scapegoating is, it confers advantages to its practitioners. For one, it rallies the faithful against an enemy portrayed as depraved and dangerous. That's how Hitler and his gang of thugs aroused the German nation against the Jews."[22] Patai expands on this idea by writing that in the Arab world, the motivation to behave honorably stems not from "guilt but [from] shame, or, more precisely,

[19] Raphael Patai, *The Arab Mind* (NY: Hatherleigh Press, 2002), 82-90.

[20] Bernard Lewis, "What Went Wrong," *The Atlantic* (January 2002), under "Terrorism," http://www.atlantic/ doc/200201/lewis (accessed January 2010).

[21] Lawrence Wright, "The Rebellion Within: An Al Qaeda Mastermind Questions Terrorism," *The New Yorker,* June 2, 2008, 24.

[22] Amil Imani, "Jews as Scapegoats," *Jihad Watch,* http://amilimani.com/index.php?option=com _context&taskb=view&id=175&Itemid=2 (accessed March 2010).

the psychological drive to escape or prevent negative judgment by others." He adds that "[c]ompared to the value of honor, that of a human life was minor."[23] Therefore, when leaders of the global jihadist movement blame the West for the ills of the Muslim world, their audiences frequently receive the message with open arms.

Patai also explains that the Arabs believe the Bedouin to be the ideal Arab archetype. Just as many Americans still honor the image of the rugged individual, many Arabs retain the Bedouin ethos as the ideal personality trait. Patai writes, "[t]he Bedouins are looked upon as images and figures from the past, as living ancestors, as latter-day heirs and witnesses to the ancient glory of the heroic age."[24] If this is true, then perhaps the West's derisive suggestion that they have pushed bin Laden and his ilk into living their lives in caves may strike the wrong cord with the Arab audience. While the West intends to denigrate him as one reduced to an unfavorable and unattractive situation, this may evoke exactly the opposite reaction from a culture that glamorizes the rugged lifestyle of the Bedouin people. Thomas L. Friedman summarizes this aspect of the Arab culture, observing that ". . . one can still find such tribe-like conflicts at work in the Middle East today [because] most peoples in this part of the world, including Israeli Jews, have not fully broken from their primordial identities, even though they live in what now appear on the surface to be modern nation-states."[25]

This ongoing connection with a "primordial identity" potentially further glamorizes the hardships faced by bin Laden. Additionally, the Arab sense of timelessness may even more deeply intertwine bin Laden with the heroic figures of the past. Patai adds, "Among the Arabs, with their typical ahistoricity [sic], the heroic age is actually timeless. . . Looking back upon the heroic ancestors, the progeny tends to endow them with almost superhuman traits, transforming them into veritable giants of courage, statesmanship, intellect, or whatever features are most

---

[23] Patai, 113, 224.

[24] Ibid., 78,82.

[25] Thomas L. Friedman, *From Beirut to Jerusalem* (New York: Anchor Books, 1990), 91.

valued in the culture of their descendants."[26] Since this recursive perception of time differs from the generally linear Western notion, what may seem like ancient history to a Westerner may be very relevant and timeless to an Arab.[27] The tradition of oral history still very prevalent in the Arab world further amplifies the timeless appeal of the rugged folk hero.

The belief in fatalism, or rather, in Allah's interplay with their daily and predestined lives, also takes center stage in the Arab value system. Patai writes, "In contrast to the West, the Arab world still sees the universe running its predestined course, determined by Allah, who not only guides the world at large, but also predestines the fate of each and every man individually."[28] Travelers in the Middle East quickly learn the ubiquitous Arabic term, *inshallah*, meaning, "if Allah wills." This belief can lead its proponents to abdicate responsibility for their actions or misgivings. Insurgency leaders may also exploit this belief to promote an agenda. For instance, Arab military defeats at the hands of the Israelis suggest that Allah is punishing the Arabs; therefore, Arabs clearly must become more Islamic to win back his favor. Writing about the events surrounding the Israeli War of Independence in 1948, Bernard Lewis explains, "[I]t was humiliating enough to be defeated by the great imperial powers of the West; to suffer the same fate at the hands of a contemptible gang of Jews was intolerable. Anti-Semitism and its image of the Jew as a scheming, evil monster provided a soothing antidote."[29] An equally soothing antidote, it would seem is the promise of reward in the afterlife for dedicated serve to jihad in the name of Allah.

---

[26] Patai, 78-79.

[27] Sarah E. Zabel, *The Military Strategy of Global Jihad* (Carlisle, PA: U.S. Army War College, 2007), 2. In her study, LTC Zabel explained that men such as Abu-Mus'ab al-Suri, a strategic thinker for the jihadist movement, believe that the Western crusades are alive and well. She states that al-Suri claimed that the "Second Crusade began with Napoleon's occupation of Egypt in 1798 and ended with the collapse of Arab nationalism in the 1970s. . . . [T]he Third Crusader Campaign began in 1990 and continues to the present time."

[28] Patai, 157.

[29] Bernard Lewis, "What Went Wrong," *The Atlantic* (January 2002), under "terrorism," http://www.theatlantic.com/doc/200201/lewis (accessed February 2010).

Additionally, the failure of the West – especially America – to kill or capture bin Laden, diminishes America's prestige in the eyes of Arabs from two perspectives. The faithful think that it is further proof that Allah is protecting bin Laden from the infidels, and secular Arabs feel emboldened to turn against the West based on what they see as years of Western incompetence. In a 2004 article, titled "The Long Hunt for Osama," al Qaeda expert Peter Bergen notes, "every day that bin Laden remains at liberty is a propaganda victory for al-Qaeda."[30] Unfortunately, what was true three years after 9/11 is still true in 2010. Capturing or killing bin Laden would be a significant blow for al Qaeda and a big victory for the West. It is unlikely that the group will disintegrate – someone will move to take his position – and his death would not magically solve all of the grievances and anger. Regardless, his personal stature and the connections and loyalties that he has secured and developed over the last three decades of jihad will be very difficult, if not impossible to replace. Additionally, as with many situations where there is a sudden power vacuum, there possibly would be an internal struggle for his position at the top of al Qaeda. The West must be prepared to exploit this opportunity when it presents itself.

This preceding section of the paper highlights some of the values and beliefs that shape the Arab Muslim world view. The following section provides a brief overview of the historical developments that shaped and influenced the contentious relationship between the Middle East and the Western world today. With an understanding of the historic narrative prevalent throughout the Middle East, one can better understand the predominant Arab perspective and anticipate how that part of the world will receive U.S. action and foreign policy.

---

[30] Peter Bergen, "The Long Hunt for Osama," *The Atlantic* (October 2004), under "Terrorism," http://www.theatlantic.com/magazine/archive/2004/10/the-long-hunt-for-osama/3508/ (accessed February 23, 2010). Bergen also notes that just five months after the 9/11 attacks, the Chairman of the Joint Chiefs, General Richard Myers, flatly stated, "I wouldn't call [getting bin Laden] a prime mission."

The Historical Narrative

The U.S. Army Field Manual, FM 3-24 *Counterinsurgency*, defines "narrative" as the following:

> A simple, unifying, easily expressed story or explanation that organizes people's experience and provides a framework for understanding events. Nationalist and ethnic historical myths and sectarian creeds are examples of such narratives. Insurgents often try to use the local narrative to support their cause. Undercutting their influence requires exploiting an alternative narrative. An even better approach is tapping into an existing narrative that excludes insurgents. [31]

To understand the Arab Muslim narrative, one must have a basic sense of their perception of history. Crucial in this endeavor is an understanding of the fall of the Ottoman Empire, the last Islamic caliphate, and the resulting exploitation of its pieces by Western powers and or Western-backed regimes. In *The Middle East and the West*, Bernard Lewis describes the importance of the last caliphate, describing the Ottoman Empire as ". . . the last and the most enduring of the great Islamic universal empires that had ruled over the Middle East since the day when the first of the caliphs succeeded the last of the prophets."[32]

The beginning of the end of the Ottoman Empire came at the hands of Western powers in the seventeenth century. Weakened by military defeats, the Ottomans added insult to injury by developing an economic dependence on Western capital. Lacking sufficient capital of their own, the Ottomans necessarily sought loans to build modern infrastructure. European nations, especially industrialized France and England, had an interest in expanding their markets eastward, and thus loaned them the money. J.W. Smith, a professor of economics, maintains that the loans "were granted on guarantees, concessions, and security arrangements. Banks, railways, mining

---

[31] FM 2-24, *Counterinsurgency* (Washington D.C.: Department of the Army, 2006), A-7.

[32] Lewis, *The Middle East and the West*, 72.

companies and forestry, gas and water works were all foreign built, run and owned."[33] In the age of colonialism and mercantilism, foreign powers openly began sucking the wealth out of the Ottoman caliphate. The Ottoman's decision to join the Central Powers in World War I was the final blow to the struggling Ottoman Empire. With the defeat of the Central Powers, the Ottoman Empire lay prostrate as the victorious nations divided up the Middle East.

Since the collapse of the empire and the subsequent disseverment of the last caliphate in 1924, Muslims have wrestled with the question of how they would govern themselves. One cannot overstate the significance of this loss of the caliphate. Bernard Lewis writes, "By the sixteenth century Ottoman rule, suzerainty, or influence extended over almost all of the lands of Arabic speech. Their return to political independence, after an eclipse of nearly a millennium, has been one of the most explosive events of the twentieth century."[34] After World War I, Britain and France determined virtually all the borders of the Arab states. The British won their mandate in Iraq, Palestine, and Transjordan, while Kuwait remained under British colonial rule. They also placed British-friendly monarchs in states such as Egypt and Jordan (Jordan's assigned monarch was a Saudi) to enforce British rule.[35] The French had their mandate in Lebanon and Syria, and maintained their colonies in Algeria, Morocco, and Tunisia.[36] Again, Lewis summarizes the historic significance of these events by stating that there have only been "two occasions when

---

[33] J.W. Smith, "The Rise and Decline of the Ottoman Empire," *Global Issues* (September 2001), under 'Ottoman Empire," http:// www.globalissues.org/article/247/the -rise-and-decline-of-the-ottoman-empire (accessed February 2010).

[34] Lewis, *The Middle East and the West*, 20. On page 101, he also states, "The idea of pan-Islamism – of a common front of the Muslims against the common threat of the Christian empires – seems to have been born among the Young Ottomans, in the eighteen sixties and seventies, and was probably in part inspired by the examples of the Germans and Italian nationalism and unification."

[35] Friedman, 13-16.

[36] J.W. Smith, "The Rise and Decline of the Ottoman Empire," *Global Issues* (September 2001), under 'Ottoman Empire," http:// www.globalissues.org/article/247/the -rise-and-decline-of-the-ottoman-empire (accessed February 2010).

outsiders have defeated and occupied the Islamic Middle East, the Mongols and the modern West."[37]

The relatively weakened nature of the newly defined Arab states made them dependant on their European sponsors. This was not by accident. Smith adds, "[w]ith centuries of mercantilist experience, Britain and France created small, unstable states whose rulers needed their support to stay in power."[38] While the colonial sponsorship made the ruling Muslim elites enormously wealthy, it left most of their citizens in poverty. Even after colonial governments lost control over Middle East in the wake of World War II, they maintained economic influence via industry, military training and sales, and finance. Throughout the Cold War to present day, America would play the most significant Western role in the Middle East. [39]

America's Role in The Arab Muslim Narrative

Not until World War II did the United States factor into the lives of ordinary Arabs. With the discovery of oil in the Arabian Peninsula in the 1930s, the oil industry, joined by postwar development efforts, introduced a steady increase of visitors, businesspersons, and eventually Western pop culture into the Arab Muslim world.[40] Many Americans did not anticipate that America would inherit the baggage of European colonialism and gain the moniker of "imperialist." However, Arabs would soon come to identify America as "the West," thus conferring upon them responsibility for the historic clash between Islam and the West. This

---

[37] Lewis, *The Middle East and the West*, 27.

[38] J.W. Smith, "The Rise and Decline of the Ottoman Empire," *Global Issues* (September 2001), under 'Ottoman Empire," http:// www.globalissues.org/article/247/the -rise-and-decline-of-the-ottoman-empire (accessed February 2010).

[39] S.K. Malik, *The Quranic Concept of War* (New Delhi, India: Himalayan Books, 1986), xx. Bin Laden's reference to the "umma," is in line with the idea of the "Umnah of Mohammad, the Profit of Islam" written in the preface of this book by Chief of the Pakistani Army Staff, General M. Zia-ul-haq, he stated that the umma. "is incapable of being realized within the framework of territorial states."

[40] Bernard Lewis, "The Roots of Muslim Rage," *The Atlantic* (September 1990), under "Muslim Rage," http://www.theatlantic.com/doc/1990/muslim-rage. (accessed February 23, 2010).

included all of the history and animosity between Christianity and Islam, Europe and the various caliphates, crusades, and imperialism. Lewis explains, "The West is seen as sexist, racist, and imperialistic; institutionalized in policies that perpetuate slavery, tyranny, and exploitation."[41] In addition to an adopted narrative, several factors added to an increasing feeling of anti-Americanism in the Middle East.

With a growing religious revival in the Muslim world in the twentieth century, led by Islamic thinkers such as Seyyid Qutb, the United States became the enemy of Allah in the eyes of many Muslims. America's support in the United Nations for the recognition of the establishment of Israel in 1948, its overt support of Israel's military capabilities beginning in 1967, and the critical logistics support the United States provided Israel during the 1973 Yom Kippur War, most likely exacerbated this perception. From that point forward, America symbolized "the West" while appearing interchangeably as either the puppet or the master of the Christian-Jewish alliance. Muslim satellite television reinforced this perception by broadcasting continuous coverage of American military operations in Muslim countries such as Iraq, Somalia, and the Balkans in the 1990s, and the GWOT since 2001. Michael Scherer, former head of the CIA's bin Laden unit, writes that "[a]ll Muslims would see each day on television that the U.S. was occupying a Muslim country, insisting that man-made laws replace God's revealed word, stealing Iraq's oil, and paving the way for the creation of a 'Greater Israel.'"[42]

In addition, the anti-Western and anti-American propaganda campaigns of the World Wars and the Cold War had a significant effect on shaping perceptions in the Middle East. According the Bernard Lewis, long after the wars ended, many Arabs saw America as "the

---

[41] Bernard Lewis, "The Roots of Muslim Rage," *The Atlantic* (September 1990), under "Muslim Rage," http://www.theatlantic.com/doc/1990/muslim-rage (accessed February 23, 2010). Dr. Lewis goes on to say, "in having practiced sexism, racism, and imperialism, the West was merely following the common practice of mankind through the millennia of recorded history. Where it is distinct from all other civilizations is in having recognized, named, and tried, not entirely without success, to remedy these historic diseases."

[42] Michael Scheuer, *Marching Toward Hell: America and Islam After Iraq* (New York: Free Press, 2008), 217.

ultimate example of civilization without culture: rich and comfortable, materially advanced but soulless and artificial; . . . technologically complex but lacking the spirituality and vitality of the rooted, human, national cultures of the Germans and other 'authentic' peoples."[43] Lewis also explains that, ". . . [i]n the thirties and early forties Fascism and Nazism had, to many, offered a seductive alternative to Western liberalism – an ideology that combined the merits of being opposed to the Western way of life, to the Western group of powers, and of being supported by an immensely strong anti-Western military bloc."[44]

The academic world of European and American universities also unintentionally played into the anti-American message in the Middle East. In *The Roots of Muslim Rage*, Lewis describes how Western theories, mainly French and American, expressed the ideal of Third Worldism. Lewis defines "Third Worldism" as "the universal human tendency to invent a golden age in the past . . . In this case it was in the Third World, where the innocence of the non-Western Adam and Eve was ruined by the Western serpent. Goodness and purity of the East and the wickedness of the West."[45] This idea would certainly be a welcome plank in any propagandist's message platform and well received by a society eager to assign blame for their ills. It carries the credibility and legitimacy of the Western academic world, as well as being vague enough to apply to a myriad of grievances.

By the 1970s, the United States' support for Arab regimes and contentious special relationship with Israel contributed to the anti-American sentiment in the Middle East. A common Arab narrative exploited by groups like al Qaeda maintains that the West uses OPEC to control the price of oil, and that America actively prevents Muslim countries from accumulating strong economies and capital. J.W. Smith provides two examples that reinforce this perception in his

---

[43] Bernard Lewis, "The Roots of Muslim Rage," *The Atlantic* (September 1990), under "Muslim Rage," http://www.theatlantic.com/doc/1990/muslim-rage (accessed February 2010).

[44] Lewis, *The Middle East and the West*, 110.

[45] Bernard Lewis, "The Roots of Muslim Rage," *The Atlantic* (September 1990), under "Terror" http://theatlantic.com/doc/199009/muslim-rage (accessed February 2010).

essay titled, "The Rise and Decline of the Ottoman Empire." First, he details Western medaling in 1950s Iranian politics. Soon after Dr. Mohammed Mossadeq, took the reins of power in Iran from a British-backed ruler in 1951, a Western (U.S. and U.K.) backed coup removed him from power in 1953 and placed the Shah back in the position. Smith claims that the reason behind the coup stemmed from Mossadeq's intent to nationalize the Iranian oil industry.

Smith also details U.S. foreign policy designed to prevent Middle Eastern countries from accumulating wealth. He explains how Henry Kissinger, President Nixon's national security advisor, recommended that the U.S. capitalize on the flow of petrodollars going to the Middle East by selling them arms. This gives the impression that "except when allies are needed in balance of power struggles – the owners of capital have always tried to prevent the development or accumulation of competing capital, in spite of the rhetoric of compassion and aid for the world's impoverished. Purposely soaking up oil money to prevent competing centers of capital that could build industry."[46] Based on the past rumors, propaganda, and general lack of trust of the West, one can better understand why many Arabs see the 1990-1991 Persian Gulf War as another example of an attack by the West to protect the current owners of capital.

Thus far, the monograph has highlighted several key characteristics defining the culture of the Muslim world and outlining their historical grievances with the West. This perspective allows all Western participants in the GWOT, from the Commander in Chief down to the lowest-ranking soldier on the ground to understand the motivation of the enemy. They had a glorious past, and yet many Arabs have a humiliating present. Once "global" leaders in science and medicine during the height if Islam, Arabs are now distant followers at best. Muslim humiliation stems from "a growing awareness, among the heirs of an old, proud, and long dominant civilization, of having been overtaken, overborne, and overwhelmed by those whom they

---

[46] J.W. Smith, "The Rise and Decline of the Ottoman Empire," *Global Issues* (September 2001), under 'Ottoman Empire,' http:// www.globalissues.org/article/247/the -rise-and-decline-of-the-ottoman-empire (accessed February 2010).

regarded as their inferiors."[47] At the same time, many Arabs believe that, "[i]f not for the plundering of the Arab world for the last 1300 years, all societies could have progressively built their capital, and their citizens could be living in decent homes, could be educated, could have a respectable life."[48] In this way, humiliation combines with anger and blame to inspire and motivate a formidable opponent.

Simply put, when America's national strategies, policies, and messages do not reflect an understanding of the environment in question, the misunderstanding compromises the ability to obtain the desired end state. Lewis writes, "[i]n the classical Islamic view, to which many Muslims are beginning to return, the world and all mankind are divided into two: the House of Islam, where Muslim law and faith prevail, and the rest, known as the House of Unbelief or the House of War, which it is the duty of Muslims ultimately to bring to Islam."[49] Understanding the environment will help Western governments understand how al Qaeda uses and manipulates the religion, culture, narrative and situation in the Middle East.

Americans also need to comprehend how the historical narrative of the Middle East influences the way Arabs understand the world. It drives their perceptions of self and their current environment. The Arab Muslim narrative, combined with their belief in fatalism and tendency to blame others, results in a circular and at times self-destructive logic. Given this logic, they are susceptible to blaming the West for all misfortunes great and small. If Allah allows the apostate West to cause Muslims harm, their logic goes, he is apparently upset with them. Therefore, they must strive to make amends with Allah. How better to please Allah than by doing harm to the

---

[47] Bernard Lewis, "The Roots of Muslim Rage," *The Atlantic* (September 1990), http://www.theatlantic.com/magazine/archive/1990/09/the-roots-of-muslim-rage/4643/. p. 9.

[48] J.W. Smith, "The Rise and Decline of the Ottoman Empire," *Global Issues* (September 2001), under 'Ottoman Empire," http:// www.globalissues.org/article/247/the -rise-and-decline-of-the-ottoman-empire (accessed February 2010). He adds that the 1975-1976 Church Committee hearings lent credibility to the negative perspective of Western activities in the Muslim world.

[49] Bernard Lewis, "The Roots of Muslim Rage," *The Atlantic* (September 1990), http://www.theatlantic.com/magazine/archive/1990/09/the-roots-of-muslim-rage/4643/. p. 3.

West? Those who cannot wait to reap the rewards of everlasting glory can ensure their place in heaven by become a martyr or, even better, a suicide bomber.[50]

Perhaps a better understanding of these aspects of the Arab Muslim world would have led the U.S. strategy in the GWOT on a different path. The benefit of hindsight reveals the shortsightedness behind the decision to invade and occupy Iraq before a decisive defeat of al Qaeda in Afghanistan. In a Brookings Institution forum on al Qaeda in March 2010, Bruce Riedel, a thirty-year veteran of the CIA, stated, "… a lot of al Qaeda's success over the last decade has been due to [America's] mistakes: going into war in Iraq when we should have finished the war in Afghanistan being the most notable."[51] Scheuer seconds this notion and highlights the gravity of the situation. "The White House and Congress," he asserts, "should have recognized that it was daft to start a second infidels-attack-Islam war that would ensure that the first would be irretrievably lost, and that would speed the transformation of bin Laden and al-Qaeda from a man and an organization into a philosophy and a world-wide movement."[52] Likewise, had the U.S. understood the nature of the war as an effort in counterinsurgency, the perceptions and values of the Arab Muslim world might have played a larger role in the decision to embark on exporting democracy to Iraq and the Islamic Republic of Afghanistan. "When we went into Iraq," says former Chief of Middle East Intelligence Colonel Pat Lang, "we went into the Islamic world with the basic belief that our culture was exportable in regard to political forms. . . . At the same time, we seem to have a very difficult time seeing the people who actually live there for what they are in their own terms."[53]

---

[50] Bruce Hoffman, *Inside Terrorism* (New York: Columbia University Press, 2006), 136.

[51] Bruce Riedel, "The Search for Al Qaeda: Its Leadership, Ideology, and Future," *The Brookings Institution* (March 9, 2010), under "al Qaeda," http://www.brookings.edu/events/2010/ 0309_al_qaeda. aspx.

[52] Scheuer, 122-123.

[53] Pat Lang, *Al Qaeda Now: Understanding Today's Terrorists* (New York: Cambridge University Press, 2005), 91.

The Enemy: Understanding
al Qaeda and Their Relationship with the Muslim World

Sun-Tzu famously said, ". . . one who knows the enemy and knows himself will not be endangered in a hundred engagements. One who does not know the enemy but knows himself will sometimes be victorious, sometimes meet with defeat." Of course, he finished the thought with the ominous observation that one who knows neither will, "invariably be defeated in every engagement."[54] One would hope that Sun-Tzu's sage advice has influenced the policymaking and war fighting branches of the U.S. government, as well as Western media, academia, and even the general public.

A significant and growing body of literature on the Global War on Terror exists. Biographies and histories – on bin Laden in particular or terrorism in general, on what the Quran does or does not really say, and the growing canon of books and reports criticizing the multitude of deficiencies in U.S. strategy before and after 9/11 – currently occupy a substantial section of library and bookstore shelves. Self-flagellating critiques of Abu Grab, Guantanamo Bay, torture, weapons of mass destruction, the decision to invade Iraqi, the decision to occupy Afghanistan, and the feasibility of Western powers spreading democracy in both will be a cottage industry for writers and publishers throughout the foreseeable future, as will titillating inside stories of headline-making personalities such as Clinton, Bush, Rumsfeld, Cheney, and President Obama. While self-reflection is certainly essential and relevant to the intellectual and political growth of the nation, the clamorous juxtaposition of these topics creates a cacophony of noise that distracts from the complex problem of non-state actors such as al Qaeda. In the face of that noise, this section of the monograph attempts to focus on the phenomenon of religiously motivated global jihad in general and al Qaeda in particular. Developing an effective strategy for defeating al Qaeda requires understanding the enemy, to include its origin, goals, motivation and logic.

---

[54] Sun-Tzu, *The Art of War* (Boulder, Colorado: Westview Press, 1994), 179.

Equally important is understanding which attributes of the organization contribute and detract from their appeal within the Muslim world.

Al Qaeda

Al Qaeda was created when Osama bin Laden and a small core of like-minded individuals seized an opportunity to capitalize on the environment of the Muslim world in the late 1980s. One can hardly imagine a situation better suited to the birth of an organization such as al Qaeda than the historical seam between the Cold War and post-Cold War period. While an amazed world watched as the defeated Soviet Union withdrew from Afghanistan and subsequently collapsed from within, and while the West struggled over how best to spend its perceived peace dividend in the afterglow of its stunning victory over Iraq in 1991, bin Laden focused on moving forward with his designs for a war with the West.[55] In a 2003 Foreign Affairs article, Ellen Laipson summarizes America's national security community's situation in the 1990s.

> Now that the Cold War dragon had been slain, . . . [the U.S. had to decide] which of the many snakes at America's feet deserved the most attention? Was it instability from failing states, the potential for a resurgent Russia, China's military modernization, or Islamist terrorism? In the absence of clear guidance, the national security bureaucracy did not systematically organize itself to counter one particular threat. Meanwhile, in the remote corners of the Muslim world and in the shabby suburbs of major Western cities, al Qaeda operatives displayed no such confusion. Slowly and steadily, they were building up their capabilities and cadres to expand their jihad against the West. These two parallel stories came together in tragedy on September 11, 2001.[56]

---

[55] The 1991 American-led victory in Operation Desert Storm marked the successful culmination of years of military restructuring, training, and procurement after its defeat in Vietnam. It was also the exclamation point on America's perception that it was sitting on an unchallenged position at the top of the international food chain.

[56] Ellen Laipson, "While America Slept: Understanding Terrorism and Counterterrorism," *Foreign Affairs*, January/February 2003, http://www.foreignaffairs.com/articles/58630/ellen-laipson/while-america-slept-understanding-terrorism-and-counterterrorism (accessed March 2, 2010).

Just ten years before the 9/11 attacks, the American-led coalition against Iraq in 1991 routed the fourth largest army in the world in a matter of hours, leaving no doubt that the United States enjoyed an unmatched advantage in technology, firepower, and professional military. This, in conjunction with the collapse of the Soviet Union in 1991, left the United States as the uncontested sole superpower. While it might seem counterintuitive for bin Laden to have picked a war with the West in light of its demonstrated military capabilities in the deserts of Iraq, he may not have chosen a better time. In this heady post-Cold War atmosphere, the United States did not consider the assessed risk from non-state actors or terrorist probable or significant. Therefore, it was not at the top of national security priorities. At the same time, bin Laden and his compatriots believe that they toppled the Soviet Union in Afghanistan, thus defeating what they perceived as the stronger of the two superpowers. The men behind the 9/11 attacks adroitly took advantage of this situation. Michael Scheuer notes, "[o]ur current Islamist enemies used the 1990s as a decade-long educational exercise in which they kept pushing the envelope to see how much pain they could inflict on the United States without triggering an annihilating U.S. response."[57] Although both bin Laden's group of mujahedeen and the United States believed that they had entered into a new period of prominence, only one was busy plotting against the other.

Surrounded by a cohort of battle-tested, networked, and motivated jihadists still exuberant from their victory in Afghanistan, Osama bin Laden had the raw materials needed to staff his fledgling organization. In terms of potential manpower, these fighters did not just emerge from the battlefields of Afghanistan. "Between 1982 and late 2001," writes Scheuer, "those [terrorists training camps] produced tens of thousands of well-trained terrorists and insurgents. . . . In the worst case, there could have been up to a million Islamists trained in camps around the world."[58] In terms of a ready-made cause behind which to rally, many, if not most, Middle

---

[57] Scheuer, 193.

[58] Ibid., 34-35.

Eastern governments lacked credible leadership and fell somewhere between incompetent, corrupt, and repressive. This made them and their citizens ripe for exploitation. Perhaps the last essential ingredient needed was money, and bin Laden was able to use his seemingly bottomless personal wealth to fund the organization until it became profitable on its own.[59] The geo-political situation mentioned above and the globalized and interconnected world facilitated al Qaeda's ability to operate globally and, in many ways, virtually.

With all the necessary ingredients in place, al Qaeda would soon prove impossible to ignore. Tragically, from their founding in 1988 to the American invasion of Afghanistan in October 2001, they set the terms of their introduction to the West through death, destruction and propaganda. In a contest of competence, they were already many steps ahead by the time the tragic acts of September 11, 2001, made them infamous. America's wakeup call came in the form of the smoldering ruins of the World Trade Center, the defiled Pentagon, and a scorched field in Pennsylvania. Al Qaeda proved that the formidable United States was not immune to terrorism, and that its deterrence doctrine was irrelevant against non-state actors.[60] The heightened probability of continued attacks added to the demonstrated gravity of the effects al Qaeda was capable of delivering. The situation necessitated a quick and overwhelming response. Tragically, the West appears to have been simply unable to reorganize itself quickly enough to deal effectively with al Qaeda's asymmetric and religiously motivated warfare.

Likewise, it is difficult to develop a strategy to defeat an enemy without first understanding the nature of the conflict. Despite the immense effort of sustaining combat for more than eight years, reorganizing and integrating the nation's intelligence community, and

---

[59] *The 9/11 Commission Report* indicates that al Qaeda's funding primarily came from fund-raising and that bin Laden's wealth was actually limited to a yearly allowance of one million dollars a year from 1970 to 1994. 9/11 Panel, "Al Qaeda Planned to Hijack 10 Planes," CNN (June 16, 2004), "9/11 Report," http://www.cnn.com/2004/ALLPOLITICS/06/16/911.commission/index html (accessed March 17, 2010).

[60] Scheuer, 46.

investing billions in homeland security, al Qaeda remains difficult to define and analyze.[61] This is in part because they continue to defy the combined efforts of America's technologically-oriented intelligence capabilities by simply avoiding electronic signatures, hiding amongst the people, language barriers, and competition with other national priorities. This is also in large part because the West has categorized and defined al Qaeda by many different labels: insurgents, terrorist, Islamofascists, Islamists, militant Islamists, fundamentalist, violent extremists, jihadists, mujahedeen, suicide bombers, homicide bombers, and non-state actors.[62] In reality, they are all of the above – not just one of the above.

Rather than pigeonholing them into one group or another, a more accurate description of al Qaeda would classify them as a regionally-focused Sunni Islamic insurgency that uses terror to advance its goals and has the ability to conduct operations globally. That is a mouthful, and not likely something a political candidate would want as a talking point; however, it is much more accurate than limiting al Qaeda to narrow categories, such as a terrorist group or religious fanatics. In addition, unlike the conventional threats defeated by America in the past, such as Nazi Germany, Imperial Japan, or the Soviet forces never fought, al Qaeda is a non-state actor, and as a result all too easy to dismiss, even after the events of 9/11. Consequently, a strategy to defeat al Qaeda has to account for its multiple personalities and unconventional nature.

To understand who they are, one must also understand what al Qaeda wants. Seyyid Qutb, the man considered the founder of the modern Islamist movement, is a good place to begin the exploration of al Qaeda's goals and strategy. Qutb's seminal text, published in 1964, provides a blueprint for restoring Islamic greatness. This text, titled *Milestones*, is described by Jonathan

---

[61] Even the name of the war has added confusion to the nature of the war. The war has been called the GWOT, the Long War, and even an "overseas contingency operation."

[62] In addition to the confused terminology, Washington has increasingly politicized the war itself. It does not serve the nation well when the issues of wartime strategy become planks in political platforms rather than bipartisan issues to debated, resolved, and then resourced with the full backing of the whole government and population.

Raban as ". . . the essential charter of the jihad movement - its Mein Kampf."[63] In *Milestones*, Seyyed Qutb explains, "If Islam is again to play the role of leader of mankind, then it is necessary that the Muslim community be restored to its original form."[64] His plan essentially argues that, to return the Muslim world to the true path of Islam, no other forms of government are legitimate but those based on Islamic law. Ayman al-Zawahiri echoes Qutub's ideas in his 1991 book, *The Bitter Harvest: The Muslim Brotherhood in Sixty Years,* when he writes, "It is forbidden to overthrow a tyrant, but it is a duty to overthrow an infidel." He then adds, "[T]he current rulers of Muslim countries who govern without the *sharia* of Allah are apostate infidels."[65] Therefore, in the eyes of the Islamist, tyrannies are acceptable forms of governance as long as they are not secular tyrannies.

From these texts, at least three of al Qaeda's goals emerge: to unify the people of the Muslim world; to return that world to a state of greatness under Islamic law; and to expel the infidels. Time and again, Osama bin Laden echoes each of these sentiments. For example, his message, *To the Muslims of Iraq,* written toward the end of 2002, clearly demonstrates his intention at that time to topple the regimes in the region. In preparation for the possible U.S.-led invasion, he stresses "to honest Muslims" that "in the midst of such momentous events and [in this] heated atmosphere, they must move, incite, and mobilize the Muslim umma [international community of Muslims] to liberate itself from being enthralled to these unjust and apostate ruling regimes, who themselves are enslaved to America, and to establish the sharia of Allah on

---

[63] Jonathan Raban, "Truly, Madly, Deeply Devout," *The Guardian* (March 2, 2002), under "Qutb," http://www.guardian.co.uk/education/2002/mar/02/socialsciences.highereducation (accessed March 17, 2010).

[64] Seyyed Qutb, *Milestones* (Damascus: Dar Al-Ilm, 1964), 9. Peter Bergen, in "The Long Hunt for Osama," calls Qutb, "the Lenin of the jihadist movement." He also warns that Qutb's execution in Egypt gave him more notoriety and influence in death than he had in life, and that the same may happen if bin Laden is martyred on the battlefield.

[65] Ayman al-Zwahiri, translated by Raymond Ibrahim, *The Al Qaeda Reader* (New York: Doubleday, 2007), 122.

earth."[66] This reveals al Qaeda's quest for sharia, a comprehensive body of laws governing

Islamic society, based on "commandments, prohibitions, and precedents found in the Koran and

summa," writes Raymond Ibrahim, author of *The Al Qaeda Reader*. Specifically, "[i]n Sunni

Islam, every law, practice, or ideology must ultimately be traced back to . . . the 'roots of

jurisprudence.' These are, in order of authority, the Koran, the sunna (example) of the Prophet,

the process of analogy, and consensus of the umma, especially the ulema."[67] This religiously

entrenched political agenda frequently confounds Western audiences steeped in the tradition of a

clear separation between church and state.

In order to achieve their goals, namely, reunifying the Muslim world under strict Islamic

law, expelling the infidels, and returning Arab peoples to a state of greatness, bin Laden and his

cohorts carefully crafted media messages that used logic that deliberately appealed to the people

of the Muslim world. This use of logic also served to demonize the West, which further motivated

their members and supported efforts to recruit additional followers.

For example, Qutb attempts to discredit the West's advantage in modern technology and

progress, writing, "[i]f we look at the sources and foundations of modern ways of living, it

becomes clear that the whole world is steeped in Jahiliyyah [ignorance of the Divine guidance],

and all the marvelous comforts and high-level inventions do not diminish this ignorance."[68] He

then links this logic to man-made governments stating, "This Jahiliyyah is based on rebellion

against God's sovereignty on earth. It transfers to man one of the greatest attributes of God,

namely sovereignty, and makes some men lords over others."[69] With this framework, he links the

---

[66] Osama bin Laden, translated by Raymond Ibrahim, *The Al Qaeda Reader* (New York: Doubleday, 2007), 147. "The umma is the international 'community' or 'nation' of Muslims that transcends ethnic, linguistic, and political definition." xxii.

[67] Ibrahim, xxi, 7. The term "Ulema" refers to "all the past and present scholars who have made it their business to know and study every aspect of Islam."xxii.

[68] Qutb, 10-11.

[69] Ibid., 11.

social ills of exploitation and humiliation to the "greed for wealth and imperialism [that exist] under capitalistic and communist systems" of governance. This destroys the legitimacy of all forms of secular government, regardless of how benevolent and capable, because secular government usurps God's authority. Again, al-Zawahiri echoes this same logic in the treatise, "Sharia and Democracy." In it, al-Zawahiri rails against the Muslim Brotherhood for their participation in, and thus acceptance of, the Egyptian political process. He writes that whoever "claims to be a 'democratic Muslim,' or a Muslim who calls for democracy, is like one who says about himself 'I am a Jewish Muslim,' or 'I am a Christian Muslim' – the one worse than the other. He is an apostate infidel."[70]

Those living in unsatisfactory social conditions after having been indoctrinated to accept the religious unpinning of Qutb's arguments may have an easier time accepting this argument. This is especially true when one's government is either corrupt, incompetent, or both. Unfortunately, many generations of Arab Muslims have lived under these conditions. As long as America's strategy in the GWOT includes establishing democracy in Muslim lands, American policymakers should assume that al Qaeda will continue to undermine U.S. efforts to foster democracy in the Muslim world, regardless of the benefits it may provide to its people.

A little over thirty years after the publication of *Milestones*, Osama bin Laden released his own statement in October 1996, titled, *A Declaration of Jihad against the Americans Occupying the Land of the Two Holy Sanctuaries*. In it, he identifies the occupation of Saudi Arabia as ". . . the greatest disaster to befall the Muslims since the death of the Prophet Muhammad."[71] What made the "infidel" occupation of "the cornerstone of the Islamic world" even more difficult to palate was that the Saudi royal family invited the Americans in order to

---

[70] Ibrahim, 119. Ibrahim calls al-Zawahiri, "al Qaeda's primary ideologue and theoretician," and notes that he joined the Muslim Brotherhood when he was fourteen years old, but then left the group to pursue groups that were more radical.

[71] Osama bin Laden, *Messages To The World, The Statements Of Osama Bin Laden*, ed, Bruce Lawrence (New York: Verso, 2005), 25.

protect the Kingdom from Iraqi forces staged on the Saudi/Kuwait border. This happened despite years of purchasing expensive American military equipment, bin Laden's personal warnings concerning the threat of Saddam Hussein to the Kingdom, and his personal offer to fight the Iraqis with his mujahedeen army.[72] The continued presence of American forces in the Kingdom of Saudi Arabia led bin Laden to authorize defensive jihad. He claimed that the people of Islam "have been afflicted with oppression, hostility, and injustice by the Judeo-Christian alliance and its supporters."[73] Here he tapped into the historic narrative of exploitation of Muslims by outside (namely European) powers and more modern Islamic philosophy. Bin Laden also learned from the U.S. military operations in the 1990s and began to prepare his organization appropriately.

Al Qaeda, like all insurgent groups, needs a permissive environment in order to operate effectively. They achieve this in the Middle East by capitalizing on negative social conditions, exploiting anti-American sentiment, and manipulating the meaning of religious duty required of "true" Arab Muslims. Al Qaeda's efforts also include exploiting or creating grievances, finding or creating ungoverned spaces, and appealing to Muslim values and pride through their information operations wing. They primarily create these spaces through the use of terror designed to coerce people to join their cause or get out of their way. Their most eye-catching tactic is the conduct of spectacular suicide attacks. Bruce Hoffman explains the benefits of employing these tactics, describing suicide bombings as ". . . inexpensive and effective. They are less complicated and compromising than other kinds of terrorist operations. They guarantee media coverage. The suicide terrorist is the ultimate smart bomb. Perhaps most important, coldly efficient bombings tear at the fabric of trust that holds societies together."[74] In *Dying to Win*, Robert Pape writes that suicide terrorism ". . . is the most aggressive form of terrorism, pursuing coercion even at the

[72] Lawrence Wright, *The Looming Tower: Al-Qaeda and the Road to 9/11* (New York, Alfred A. Knopf, 2006), 154-158.

[73] bin Laden, 23.

[74] Bruce Hoffman, "The Logic of Suicide Terrorism," *The Atlantic* (June 2003), under "Terrorism," http://www.theatlantic.com/doc/200306/hoffman (accessed March 17, 2010).

expense of angering not only the target community but neutral audiences as well."[75] Later in this section, the monograph will further explore the Muslim world's intolerance for al Qaeda's overuse and abuse of suicide terrorism. The main point is that groups like al Qaeda use terrorism as a tool to achieve their desired ends.

In his 2001 book, *Knights Under the Prophet's Banner*, Ayman al-Zawahiri promotes moving the battle "to the enemy's ground to burn the hands of those who ignite the fire in our countries."[76] At the same time, he suggests the most efficient method for obtaining this end, encouraging his followers to "concentrate on the method of martyrdom operations as the most successful way of inflicting the most damage against the opponent and the least costly to the mujahideen in terms of casualties."[77] The American Embassy bombings in Africa, the 9/11 attacks against the U.S., the Madrid attacks against Spain, and the London bombings all indelibly exemplify their capability to follow these instructions on an international scale.

Unfortunately, the past attacks, as heinous as they were, do not represent the worst-case terrorist scenario. This dubious honor will go to the first terrorist group willing to use a nuclear weapon in a U.S. city. One must assume that al Qaeda has this willingness. There is little doubt that they desire such a weapon. In a 2004 interview discussing nuclear terrorism, Harvard Professor Graham Allison addresses the feasibility of a terrorist group using weapons of mass destruction:

> About four months after the 9/11 attack, Osama bin Laden's press spokesman, a fellow named Abu Ghaith, put up on the al-Qaeda web site al-Qaeda's objective to "kill four million Americans, including two million children." And he goes on to explain that this is not picked out of thin air, but is the result of a gruesome calculus of what's required to "balance the scales of justice," as he sees it, for the

---

[75] Robert A. Pape, *Dying to Win: The Strategic Logic of Suicide Terrorism* (New York: Random House, 2006), 10.

[76] Bruce Hoffman, "The Logic of Suicide Terrorism," *The Atlantic* (June 2003), under "Terrorism," http://www.theatlantic.com/doc/200306/hoffman (accessed March 17, 2010).

[77] Ibid.

number of Muslims who have been killed by what he calls "the Jewish-Christian Crusaders," by which he means the Israelis and the Americans.[78]

The idea of reciprocity has long been at the foundation of bin Laden's logic behind the killing of innocent civilians. "Practically every message issued by al-Qaeda to the West revolves around the theme of 'reciprocal treatment,'" writes Ibrahim.[79] In a 1998 interview with ABC reporter John Miller, bin Laden states that, "[t]he Americans started it and retaliation and punishment should be carried out following the principle of reciprocity, especially when woman and children are involved." In the same interview, he rails against "those who threw atomic bombs and used the weapons of mass destruction [against Japan]," asking rhetorically if the bombs could "differentiate between military and woman and infants and children."[80]

Al Qaeda has also proven adept at information operations. They expertly exploit and export real and perceived grievances – old and new – through a carefully managed media campaign. Bruce Lawrence writes,

> In a period of ten years that coincide with the emergence of a virtual universe, moving from print to internet, from wired to wireless communication around the globe, bin Laden and his associates have crafted a series of carefully staged statements designed for the new media. These include interviews with Western and Arab journalists . . . and above all video recordings distributed via the first independent Arabic-language news outlet, the Qatari satellite television network al-Jazeera.[81]

The enemy purposely frames the GWOT as the latest phase of the crusades against Islam. They see it as an attack against their culture and religion. This is an especially powerful call to arms given how deeply intertwined their religion is in their daily lives, law, and governance.

---

[78] Graham Allison, "Nuclear Terrorism: The Ultimate Preventable Catastrophe," *Carnegie Council*: Transcripts (November 16, 2004), under "WMD," http/www.cceia.org/resources/transcripts/ 5049.html (accessed, March 17, 2010).

[79] Ibrahim, 6.

[80] Osama bin Laden, "Interview Osama Bin Laden," *Frontline*: Transcripts (May 1998), under "bin Laden interview," http://www.pbs.org/wgbh/pages/frontline/shows/binladen/who/interview.html (accessed March 16, 2010).

[81] bin Laden, *Messages To The World,* xi.

During a time when President Obama began publicly weighing the options to respond to General McCrystal's leaked troop request and following the eighth anniversary of the 9/11 attacks, al Qaeda's propaganda apparatus As-Sahab Media released a statement titled, "Statement to the American People," by Osama bin Laden.[82] Bin Laden covers a lot of ground in this brief message. In it, he returns to the theme of defensive jihad. He aspires to remind Americans of the reasons behind the 9/11 attacks, what took place after the attacks, and that the choice to continue the war is in the hands of Western leaders. He asserts that "we have shown and declared many times over more than two and a half decades that our dispute with you [is based on] your support for your allies; the Israeli occupiers of our land in Palestine."[83] Raymond Ibrahim notes that bin Laden and al-Zawahiri stick to a common idea in their messages to the West, stating, "their theme is always the same: al Qaeda is merely retaliating for all the injustices the West, and the United States in particular, has brought upon Muslims."[84] The intent of their information operation towards the West is likely to cause division within democratic societies by sparking debate over Western culpability and to create an appearance of legitimacy for al Qaeda's cause.

Their message to Muslim audiences however, has an altogether different tone. Rather than defensive jihad, revolving around the theme of reciprocity, Ibrahim uses translated text from bin Laden and al-Zawahiri to illustrate that ". . . bin Laden's war is total war that is not susceptible to olive branches or negotiation with the enemy." Ibrahim concludes, "Offensive jihad' – once thought to have been relegated to the dustbin of history – is defended as not only legitimate but obligatory. Muslims are exhorted to always hate, discriminate, humiliate, and debase non-Muslims."[85] Understanding how deeply al Qaeda's message has resonated with

---

[82] General McCrystal is the commander of the International Security Assistance Force (ISAF) in Afghanistan.

[83] Osama bin Laden, "Statement to the American People," Translated by NEFA Foundation www.nefafoundation.org.

[84] Ibrahim, 1.

[85] Ibid. 3.

Muslim audiences will help American policy makers formulate effective strategy. It does little good to spend resources on lines of effort that focus on extending olive branches or spreading democracy when the message is doomed to fail.

The Muslim Response to al Qaeda: Success or Failure?

In a memo dated October 16, 2003, Secretary of Defense Donald Rumsfeld flatly warns that "today, we lack metrics to know if we are winning or losing the GWOT." In the leaked memo, intended for an internal audience within the top echelon of the Department of Defense, he poses a series of strategic questions that remain relevant today: "Are we capturing, killing or deterring and dissuading more terrorists every day than the madrassas and the radical clerics are recruiting, training and deploying against us? . . . Are we winning or losing the GWOT? . . . "Is our current situation such that the harder we work, the behinder [sic] we get? [86] Perhaps the metrics needed to measure accurately Western success against al Qaeda need to come from within the Muslim world itself. Since al Qaeda depends on the Muslim population for survival, as noted above, Muslim reaction to them may be the most important measure of their success or failure. David Galula, a French officer who experienced revolutionary warfare in China, Greece, Southeast Asia, and Algeria in aftermath of WWII, writes, "If the insurgent manages to dissociate the population from the counterinsurgent, to control it physically, to get its active support, he will win the war because, in the final analysis, the exercise of political power depends on the tacit or explicit agreement of the population or, at worst its submissiveness." Galula concludes by stating, "The battle for the population is a major characteristic of the revolutionary war."[87] Focusing more directly on the evolving opinions of the Muslim population would allow the West to monitor al

---

[86] Donald Rumsfeld, "GWOT Memo," *USA Today* (May 20, 2005), under "GWOT," http://www.usatoday.com/news/washington/executive/rumsfeld-memo.htm (accessed December 15, 2009). The classified memo leaked within a week to *USA Today*.

[87] David Galula, *Counterinsurgency Warfare: Theory and Practice* (St. Petersburg, FL: Hailer Publishing, 2005), 9.

Qaeda's pulse without muddying the evaluation with conflicting cultural values, norms, and goals. To this end, this portion of the monograph explores the factors that both help and hinder al Qaeda's relationship with the Muslim world.

In the article titled, "Al-Qaida's Appeal: Understanding its Unique Selling Points," Brynjar Lia argues that "al-Qaida's continuing appeal is a result of three key factors: simple message, powerful image and global character."[88] He explains that their "simple popular message . . . resonates strongly with deeply held grievances in the Muslim world . . . that it has become the world's most feared terrorist organization . . . [and that] al-Qaida is virtually open to everyone."[89] In addition to stressing the average Muslim's accessibility to al Qaeda, Lia recognizes the effectiveness of al Qaeda's "simple message," which fundamentally centers on two key points: a consistent blaming of the west for the social problems in the Middle East, and a strict interpretation of Islam.

The first section of the monograph describes at length the prevalence of blame within the Muslim world, and the scapegoating of the West, by which bin Laden and his cohorts consistently and intentionally blame America and its allies for the social problems riddling the Middle East. As Michael Scheuer states, "Because bin Laden has successfully made U.S. foreign policy the center of the war of ideas, any Muslim who publicly argues that America should be given the benefit of the doubt is implicitly acquiescing in U.S. support for Israel, manipulation of oil prices, and support for Russia in Chechnya."[90] Scheuer concludes from this observation that "this is the reason why Americans hear so few 'moderate Muslim voices' opposing bin Laden and the Islamists; the moderates are out there and often do not approve of the Islamists' military actions, but they hate U.S. policies with just as much venom and passion as the Islamists, per the polls by

---

[88] Lia, 3.

[89] Ibid.

[90] Scheuer, 207-208.

Pew, Gallop, BBC, and Zogby."[91] However, their ability to place blame successfully upon the West is only one of the factors acting in al Qaeda's favor.

Understanding al Qaeda's appeal within the Muslim world also requires the examination of their religious objectives, supported widely at least within the sizeable international Sunni population. As noted above, al Qaeda fundamentally seeks the restoration of authentic Islam.[92] One can find this version of Islam, based on a strict interpretation of Koranic scripture, in Madrassas and Mosques across the globe. While they are extreme in their beliefs, words, and actions, one cannot say that the followers of al Qaeda are not devout Muslims. Nor is their message unique or unfamiliar. Their message easily manipulates common Arab grievances based on historical fact and ideological beliefs supported by Arab propensities. Their goals are also not farfetched, as evidenced by the fact that, by the time of the 9/11 attacks, three Muslim nations had already succumbed to militant Islam: Iran, Sudan, and Afghanistan.[93] "The Arabs constitute one nation, the Arab nation," observes Patai, "and the division of the one Arab fatherland into numerous separate countries is but a temporary condition that sooner or later must be, will be, overcome."[94]

After 9/11, the Bush administration clearly acknowledged al Qaeda's goals for a unified caliphate. In a 2006 speech, President Bush states,

> [The terrorists] hope to establish a violent political utopia across the Middle East, which they call a 'Caliphate' – where all would be ruled according to their hateful ideology. Osama bin Laden has called the 9/11 attacks – in his words – 'a great step towards the unity of Muslims and establishing the Righteous… [Caliphate].' This Caliphate would be

---

[91] Scheuer, 208. An important aspect of COIN is that the counterinsurgent attempts to establish and maintain legitimate authority, not necessarily popularity.

[92] Marc Segeman, *Understanding Terror Networks* (Philadelphia, PA: University of Pennsylvania Press, 2004), 1.

[93] Jonathan Schanzer, "At War With Whom: A Short History of Radical Islam," *Doublethink*, Spring 2002, http://www.meforum.org/168/at-war-with-whom (accessed April 18, 2010).

[94] Patai, 14.

a totalitarian Islamic empire encompassing all current and former Muslim lands, stretching from Europe to North Africa, the Middle East, and Southeast Asia.[95]

The President's message, however, seemingly fails to recognize that many Muslims who have nothing to do with terrorism or al Qaeda see the caliphate as a legitimate and positive entity. Unfortunately, few Muslims, especially those living in Muslim nations at the time of the President's speech, were likely to side with the Bush administration in the wake of occupation and fumbling policies in Iraq.

As the people of the Muslim world determine to whom they should be pledging their allegiance, al Qaeda or the West, al Qaeda is the "home team." In a competition between al Qaeda and many of the repressive and or corrupt Middle East regimes, al Qaeda at least has been true to its agenda and decrees. For Muslims who have not actually experienced living under the Taliban or al Qaeda in Iraq, Sharia law may sound like a legitimate plan compared to corruption and chaos. In discussing the resignation Muslims may feel to accepting this political course, Friedman harkens back to an ancient Arabic proverb, which suggests, "Better sixty years of tyranny than one day of anarchy."[96] In light of this Arab emphasis to maintain order, one must wonder how the Arab world received Secretary of Defense Rumsfeld's 2003 answer to a question concerning looting in Iraq after U.S. forces toppled the regime. He parried the issue, stating, "[s]tuff happens! . . . freedom's untidy. And free people are free to make mistakes and commit crimes and do bad things."[97]

Additionally, bin Laden continues to lead by personal example in a region that is in many ways a leadership vacuum. Michael Scheuer writes the following about bin Laden:

---

[95] George W. Bush, "President Discusses Global War on Terror," Capital Hilton Hotel, September 5, 2006, http://www.whitehouse/news/releases/2006/09//20060905-4.gov

[96] Friedman, 94.

[97] Editors, "A Nation at War; Rumsfeld's Words on Iraq: 'There is untidiness,'" *New York Times Online* (April 12, 2003), under "Rumsfeld," http://www.nytimes.com/2003/04/12/world/a-nation-at-war-rumsfeld-s-words-on-iraq-there-is-utidiness html (accessed April 15, 2010). He ultimately asserts the freedom of Iraqis to choice their destiny, but given the differences in perceptions, that nuance was likely lost.

Our Saudi foe's appeal comes not only from his eloquence, strategic vision, patience, combat record, and management skills, though he has all of those in ample measure. The astounding breadth and durable appeal of bin Laden and his message also owe much to the near-absolute lack of popular and credible leaders in the Muslim world, from Morocco to Malaysia. In a crowd of dictators, absolute monarchs, effete princes, and coup-installed generals, bin Laden was like the unexpected cream that gradually but inevitably rose to the top of Islam's bottle of fat-free milk.[98]

Since his early twenties, bin Laden has exemplified the pious warrior, first pitted against the Soviets, then as a strategist against the American-led West. He did this despite his family's incredible wealth and personal ties with the Saudi royal family. If he had just accepted the status quo and let his life follow a traditional and predictable course, he would have been another Saudi millionaire living without any of the physical hardships and sacrifices that a life on the run must require. Moreover, he has been more successful than any Arab nation state at standing up to the West, and he has been doing it for more than fourteen years.

Another strength of al Qaeda and its affiliated groups is its ability to provide an outlet for the disenchanted and disenfranchised. According to Bernard Lewis, "Islamic fundamentalism has given an aim and a form to the otherwise aimless and formless resentment and anger of the Muslim masses at the forces that have devalued their traditional values and loyalties and, in the final analysis, robbed them of their beliefs, their aspirations, their dignity, and to an increasing extent even their livelihood."[99] Whether a young Muslim male simply desires glory and adventure in this world or the promise of seventy virgins in the next, jihad under bin Laden's banner might remain an appealing beacon.

---

[98] Scheuer, 214.

[99] Bernard Lewis, "The Roots of Muslim Rage," *The Atlantic* (September 1990), http://www.theatlantic.com/magazine/archive/1990/09/the-roots-of-muslim-rage/4643/ (accessed March 2010), 9.

Western involvement in the Middle East may not be the optimal solution to stem the tide of radical Islam. Lewis explains how the West in general and America in particular can at times be al Qaeda's unintended best friend:

> Western political institutions and ideas have been discredited by Muslim reformers . . . who were operating in a situation beyond their control, using imported and inappropriate methods that they did not fully understand. . . . For vast numbers of Middle Easterners, Western-style economic methods brought poverty, Western-style political institutions brought tyranny, even Western-style warfare brought defeat. It is hardly surprising that so many were willing to listen to voices telling them that the old ways were best and that their only salvation was to throw aside the pagan innovations of the reformers and return to the True Path that God had prescribed for his people.[100]

While Lewis made this observation twenty years ago, it certainly applies to today's situation in Iraq and Afghanistan. As Washington begins slowly backing away from the fledgling democracy in Baghdad while doubling down on the Karzai government in the Islamic Republic of Afghanistan, one has to ask if these governments are on the threshold of something truly transformative, or if they are instead following the path of past reformers. Discrediting the GWOT, especially America's effort to turn the unpopular invasion of Iraq into a positive outcome, is vital to al Qaeda's future.

Fortunately for the West, and for those Muslims who do not ascribe to militant Islam, al Qaeda also has exploitable weaknesses. First, al Qaeda may have fatally miscalculated America's response to the 9/11 attacks. Bin Laden reveals their erroneous evaluation, believing that "our boys [al Qaeda elements in Somalia] were shocked by the low morale of the American soldier and they realized that the American soldier was just a paper tiger. He was unable to endure the strikes that were dealt to his army, so he fled."[101] Bin Laden concludes that America would not be

---

[100] Bernard Lewis, "The Roots of Muslim Rage," *The Atlantic* (September 1990), http://www.theatlantic.com/magazine/archive/1990/09/the-roots-of-muslim-rage/4643/ (accessed March 2010) 9.

[101] Osama bin Laden, "Interview Osama bin Laden," *Frontline*: Transcripts (May 1998), under "bin Laden Interview," http://www.pbs.org/wgbh/pages/frontline/shows/binladen/who/interview.html (accessed March 16, 2010).

up for the task of fighting his type of war, concluding, "We have seen in the last decade the decline of the American government and the weakness of the American soldier. He is ready to wage cold wars but unprepared to fight hot wars."[102] If they assumed that the withdrawal of troops after the Marine barracks bombing in Beirut in 1983 and the loss of eighteen rangers in Mogadishu in 1993 would predict the West's response to the surprise attack on 9/11, they must not have been familiar with WWII American history. Likewise, bin Laden may have overestimated how long Muslim societies would tolerate war, especially a protracted war in which more innocent Muslims would die at the hands of jihadists than would Western soldiers.

The indiscriminate killing of innocent civilians also weakens, if not destroys, al Qaeda's legitimacy throughout the Muslim world. They attempt to explain away civilian casualties, especially Muslim casualties, using Takfir logic. According to Sherifa Zuhur, a noted author on Islam, "Takfir is a method by which radicals or extremely devout Muslims declare other Muslims to be unbelievers, or those who follow kufr [disbelief in Islam]."[103] By this line of logic, these unbelievers appear to be enemies of Islam, and thus deserve to die. This argument is wearing thin, especially since al Qaeda's leadership lacks real religious authority.[104] The open criticism of their use of Takfir by the theory's architect, Sayyid Imam al-Sharif, also known as Dr. Fadl, greatly undermines al Qaeda's logic and credibility. According to Lawrence Wright, "Fadl was one of the first members of al Qaeda's top council. Twenty years ago he wrote two of the most important books in modern Islamist discourse; al Qaeda used them to indoctrinate recruits and justify killing."[105]

---

[102] Jonathan Schanzer, "At War With Whom: A Short History of Radical Islam," *Doublethink*, Spring 2002, http://www.meforum.org/168/at-war-with-whom (accessed April 18, 2010).

[103] Sherifa Zuhur, "Precision in the GWOT: Inciting Muslims through the War of Ideas," April 2008. http://www.strategicstudiesinstitute.army.mil/ (accessed March 20. 2010).

[104] Wright, 287.

[105] Lawrence Wright, "The Rebellion Within: An Al Qaeda Mastermind Questions Terrorism," *The New Yorker,* June 2, 2008, 24.

The wanton killing of civilians and harsh enforcement of rules in western Iraq led to the most significant strategic losses al Qaeda has suffered to date, with Sunni Arabs turning to the American occupation forces to rid themselves of the al Qaeda menace. While the Sunni Awakening was certainly a marriage of convenience, it set a series of events in motion that may lead to American forces leaving Iraq on-schedule and without a significant al Qaeda presence in the country. A *Los Angeles Time* article reports, "the criticism apparently has grown serious enough that al Qaeda's chief strategist Ayman al-Zawahiri, felt compelled to solicit online questions. . . . For more than 90 minutes, bin Laden's second-in-command tried to defuse the anger."[106] Brynjar Lia adds, "In recent years public outrage against al Qaeda-related violence has become more visible. There have, for example, been mass demonstrations in Jordan and Morocco against al Qaeda following terrorist attacks by al Qaeda-related groups."[107]

Lastly, al Qaeda clearly lacks an acceptable replacement for the governments they are trying to destroy. Afghanistan under the Taliban and Anbar province in western Iraq under al Qaeda are examples that reveal their tendency to govern through brutality and oppression. Their operations offer death and destruction to friend and foe alike. "At the end of the day, all jihadist terrorists can really do is kill. But the more they kill, the more they alienate their fellow Muslims" writes Peter Beinart in 2005. [108] America can and should capitalize on this weaknesses with the same dedication al Qaeda display in their goal of attacking everything that falls outside of their narrow realm of tolerance.

---

[106] Josh Meyer, "Onetime Al Qaeda loyalists now fault it," *Los Angeles Times*, April 24, 2008. http://articles.latimes.com/2008/apr/24/world/fg-qaeda24 (accessed March 27, 2010).

[107] Lia, 7.

[108] Obama Outsmarts the Terrorists, Peter Beinart, re http://www.thedailybeast.com/blogs-and-stories/2010-02-05/the-dirty-secret-of-the-terror-war/?cid=bs:featured1 (accessed March 2010).

Conclusion

This monograph began by asking why the combined forces of the various coalition powers, led by the U.S. military, have failed to defeat al Qaeda, a non-state actor virtually unheard of by most Americans until 9/11. It has asserted that an incomplete understanding of the enemy and the operational environment is critically hampering the efforts of the United States and its allies in the GWOT. The purpose of the paper has been to shed light on some of the cultural, historical, and social issues that define both al Qaeda and the Arab Muslim world—issues that policy makers and strategic planners from the West must better understand. One might think that the findings of this inquiry come too late into the war; after all, the military has already begun its efforts to pull all U.S. troops out of Iraq, and President Obama has indicated that he intends to begin reducing forces in Afghanistan in June 2011.[109] Unfortunately, al Qaeda still very much remains a threat to American national security, so much so that Admiral Mullen, the top ranking officer in the United States' military, recently told troops heading to Afghanistan that, "[w]e are not winning, which means we are losing and as we are losing, the message traffic out there to recruits keeps getting better and better and more keep coming."[110] Therefore, the topic of this monograph sadly is just as relevant today as it was when America entered the war against al Qaeda more than eight years ago. The research in this monograph has revealed several important factors about the operational environmental, the enemy and their relationship towards one another.

First, this paper highlighted the unique challenge America faces in defeating an enemy such as al Qaeda. America's strategic problem since September 11, 2001 has been how to best

---

[109] Sheryl G. Stolberg and Helene Cooper, "Obama Adds Troops, but Maps Exit Plan," *New York Times*, December 1, 2009.

[110] Jake Tapper, "Adm. Mullen Rallies U.S. Troops: 'Slope on This Insurgency Is Going in the Wrong Direction,'" *Political Punch,* December 11, 2009. http://blogs.abcnews.com/politicalpunch/ 2009/12/adm-mullen-rallies-us-troops-slope-on-this-insurgency-is-going-in-the-wrong-direction.html (accessed April 2010).

respond to a non-state actor with Cold War-era tools, ideas, and doctrine. Although 9/11 was not the first time enemy forces conducted a surprise attack against the U.S. on U.S. soil, the options available in 2001 were fundamentally different from those at hand after the attacks on Pearl Harbor, sixty years earlier. Certainly, al Qaeda had to be defeated. Yet, it was not an enemy that readily lent itself to targeting by U.S. forces. [111] It was not a nation state. It had no real army for America's military to fight, and in many ways – by both design and necessity – it was invisible to the West's technologically-driven, and dependant, intelligence capabilities. Additionally, few Americans understood al Qaeda, Islam, or the Muslim world. Therefore, it was with little in-depth knowledge of the enemy, the nature of the war, or the human terrain, that the Global War on Terror began.

After describing the unique challenge of fighting al Qaeda, the paper highlighted the importance of understanding the operational environment of the Arab Muslim world. The information discussed included the key values, norms, and beliefs found within the Arab culture, the Muslim world's historic narrative and grievances, and the effect that enemy propaganda and anti-American sentiment have had on shaping the perceptions and beliefs of Middle Eastern populations. This knowledge is important for a myriad of reasons, not the least being that both al Qaeda and America continue to fight for credibility and legitimacy in the Middle East. Both sides desire a permissive environment; al Qaeda requires it. [112] This asymmetrical requirement should be one of the focal points of American strategy to defeat al Qaeda. However, in order to achieve

---

[111] Wright, 282-285. Lawrence Wright details how America's ineffective response to the two embassy bombings in east Africa in 1998, actually benefited bin Laden. Not only did the seventy-nine Tomahawk cruise missiles (at a million dollars each) fail to kill bin Laden or dissuade al Qaeda, Wright notes that, "Sudan lost one of its most important manufactures . . . [the strikes] established bin Laden as a symbolic figure of resistance . . . [and] bin Laden sold the unexploded missiles to China for more than $10 million." For a devout Muslim such as bin Laden, these strikes must have been further proof that Allah was on his side. As a military planner, this event must have been further evidence that America was a paper tiger.

[112] Ibid. 250-255. In today's globalized world, a permissive environment does not require the occupation of large tracts of land. Many aspects of the 9/11 attacks were conceived and planned in Europe and the U.S –the pilot's flight training occurred in U.S. flight schools. Warzones, such as Iraq and Afghanistan provide more than adequate training facilities for jihadist groups.

victory, American policymakers and strategists must first understand the environment. After nearly nine years of conducting an expensive and divisive war, American can ill-afford to have anything other than an effective, culturally-aware, historically-informed plan to move forward in the GWOT.

Additionally, American policy makers and strategists must understand, prioritize, and focus on al Qaeda because of the clear and present danger this regional insurgency poses to the interests and security of the United States and its allies. The GWOT cannot sustain or repeat the meandering route taken thus far. Even a nation as economically and militarily strong as the United States has limits. For the U.S. to be able to shape its desired foreign policy and national interests in "an era of persistent conflict," America has to be judicious with its small, but expensive all volunteer force.[113] OEF and OIF have left the nation with few reserve forces to focus on any other theater or respond to unforeseen crisis. With increasing tensions with Iran over its nuclear program, the unpredictability of North Korea, and the deteriorating security situation in Mexico, America needs to rebalance its commitments. However, these rebalancing efforts cannot appear to give al Qaeda a victory. Therefore, America and its allies must unequivocally defeat al Qaeda.

At the same time, achieving this unequivocal victory requires more than killing or capturing al Qaeda's leadership. "Over the past few years, we've nailed two-thirds of the terrorists on our to-do list in the Afghanistan/Pakistan border area," boasts columnist Ralph Peters.[114] These strikes are likely an important part of the strategy to defeat al Qaeda, and certainly force the enemy to focus on force protection rather than offensive operations. Yet decapitation strikes cannot be *the* strategy. Al Qaeda has proven resilient enough to absorb these heavy losses. In

---

[113] George W. Casey, *2009 Army Posture Statement*, http://www.army.mil/aps/09/2009_army_posture_statement_web.pdf 1 (accessed March 2010).

[114] Ralph Peters, "Terrorizing Terrorists," *New York Post* (February 4, 2010), under "Terrorism," http://www.nypost.com/p/news/opinon/opedcolumnists/terrorizing_terrorists_2DSSsUhLN70IZRRLIK (accessed March 14, 2010).

addition, the U.S. must avoid falling into the perception trap that bin Laden laid in anticipation of the war he sought with America. Scheuer writes that up to six years before the 9/11 attacks,

> Osama bin Laden and Ayman al-Zawahiri conducted an education program that taught Muslims what to expect in terms of future U.S. actions in the Islamic world. The United States would, they predicted, seek to destroy strong Muslim governments and replace them with 'U.S. agent regimes.' It would forbid or replace Islamic law and put man-made law, elections, and parliaments in its place, as well as destroy any Muslim regime deemed threatening to Israel, seek to control Muslim oil resources, and occupy or destroy Islamic holy sites.[115]

With this in mind, one can see how Operation Enduring Freedom and Operation Iraq Freedom have played into the hands of al Qaeda's propaganda wing. America needs a comprehensive strategy to defeat al Qaeda as an insurgency, eroding the organization's causes, resources, and motivating factors in addition to attacking the organization itself. Jessica Stern agrees that the West must begin to attack tomorrow's terrorists, suggesting that ". . . we are making a very profound error in focusing almost exclusively on today's terrorists rather than on who becomes a terrorist and why."[116] Unfortunately, this has yet to happen in the GWOT – which threatens to be the longest of America's wars. Within the scope of such a long-term war, Stern asserts, "we need another strategy [than a military strike]. And that strategy probably has to do with undoing the misapprehension that the U.S. is deliberately out to humiliate the Muslim world."[117]

In addition, the West must begin to recognize and understand other forms of power and legitimacy besides Westphalian nation states. Non-state actors, whether al Qaeda-like organizations or super-empowered individuals likely will have a increasingly important role in shaping international relations for the foreseeable future.[118] At the historic intersection of

---

[115] Scheuer, 128-129.

[116] Jessica Stern, cited in *Al Qaeda Now: Understanding Today's Terrorists*, Karen J. Greenberg, Ed. (New York: Cambridge University Press, 2005), 36.

[117] Ibid., 39.

[118] Thomas L. Friedman, "Longitudes and Attitudes: Exploring the World After September 11," *Thomas L. Friedman.com* (2002), http://www.thomaslfriedman.com/bookshelf/longitudes-and-attitudes/prologue (accessed May 5, 2010).

globalization and the end of the Cold War, nation states simply failed to pay adequate attention to non-state actors in general, and to al Qaeda in particular. Despite the growing lethality and frequency of terror attacks in the 1990s, the U.S. did little beyond law enforcement efforts and ineffective missile strikes to defeat this threat in its embryonic stage. The lack of national prioritization and imagination resulted in a cascading series of problems that ultimately left the United States ignorant of the threat and unprepared to respond effectively to the attacks of September 11th. The U.S. must take measures to avoid making the same mistake twice.

One must also ask if the efforts to export democracy to these two Muslim countries, within the tolerance of Americans' time, effort, and money, will lead to significant erosion in support from the Muslim Arab community for al Qaeda and groups like them. Can America afford to wait long enough to reap the benefits of such ambitious but indirect programs as nation building and exporting democracy to Iraq and the Islamic Republic of Afghanistan? Americans have already paid a high price in blood and treasure from waging more than eight years of inconclusive war – spending billions of dollars trying to stabilize the situation in Iraq and Afghanistan, mourning the lives of over 5,400 American dead, and caring for more than 36,000 wounded. [119] One must ask if the goal of exporting democracy to the Middle East in an effort to rid the world of tyranny is achievable and appropriate, given these high costs. "It is the policy of the United States to seek and support democratic movements and institutions in every nation and culture, with the ultimate goal of ending tyranny in our world," suggested President Bush in 2006. [120] Those goals were certainly appropriate in the Cold War against the Soviet Union. But they may not be as appropriate if the desire for democracy is not organic to the people of the Arab Muslim world. As noted throughout the paper, the perception of American imperialism is alive

---

[119] "Casualty Update," United States Department of Defense, under "News," then "Press Releases," then "Casualty Update." http://www.defense.gov/ (accessed April 28, 2010).

[120] George W. Bush, "The National Security Strategy of The United States of America, 2006," under "NSS 2006," http://georgewbush-whitehouse.archives.gov/nsc/nss/2006/ (accessed January 4, 2010).

and well and actively promoted by al Qaeda and America's foes alike. In addition, American policymakers should be aware that Islamic thinkers such as Seyyid Qutb and those who have followed in his footsteps have spent the last forty-plus years framing democracy as an affront to Islam. The jihadist movement did not begin, nor has it grown in strength over the last few decades, because of a lack of democratic institutions in the Middle East. Their reasons, and goals have been abundantly clear in their written and spoken words. The West just has to begin listening.

Finally, America's leaders have to lead their constituents to face the fact that, because of the clear and present danger al Qaeda poses to the U.S. and its allies, and because of the vital energy resources in the Middle East, neither can be ignored nor wished away. Nor can America's involvement with the Middle East and its war against al Qaeda end on the enemy's terms. America cannot live with or deter al Qaeda as it did with the Soviets during the Cold War. America cannot negotiate an acceptable ceasefire with al Qaeda as it did with North Korea in 1953. Nor can America walk away from a war with al Qaeda as it did with Vietnam, Beirut, and Somalia. This enemy feeds on perceived weakness and, and it will follow U.S. forces home. Instead, America must win a decisive victory against this ruthless and determined enemy.

Understanding and articulating what that victory might look like should be one of America's primary goals in the war against al Qaeda. This will require a break from the past, moving forward with a deeper understanding of the operational environment and the enemy. America must align its policies and strategies with a sound understanding of the environment as it is and the enemy it faces today. Since the enemy is an insurgent movement against the regimes in the Middle East, America cannot win the war for them, especially if those states lack legitimacy and authority within their borders. "A victory is not the destruction in a given area of the insurgent's forces and his political organization," writes David Galula, on achieving victory in counterinsurgency warfare. "If one is destroyed, it will be locally re-created by the other; if both are destroyed, it will both be re-created by a new fusion of insurgents from the outside." He goes on to say, "A victory is that plus the permanent isolation of the insurgent from the population, isolation not enforced upon the population but maintained by and with the population."[121] The U.S. must heed this advice and refrain from continuing on a never-ending cycle of operational whack-a-mole followed by expensive and lengthy nation building based on the idea of defeating al Qaeda – and all tyranny – with exported democracy.

Al Qaeda's downfall will likely come at the hands of fellow Muslims, not American bombs and occupation forces. As the paper has detailed, al Qaeda has significant flaws that its foes should exploit. They have killed more of their fellow Muslims than Western forces, and have little to offer in terms of governance than a brutally enforced and oppressive way of life.[122] An understanding of the Arab Muslim world also includes a history rich in culture, science, and education that would never have accepted bin Laden's vision of the world. Whatever direction the GWOT takes, America cannot afford to let al Qaeda think it won another war with a superpower. The effects of such a victory are not unimaginable.

---

[121] Galula, 77.

[122] Wright, 230-231.Wright notes that the Taliban severely enforced outlawed activities such as, "kite flying," and forbade items such as, "anything made from human hair . . . cinematography . . . any equipment that produces the joy of music . . . chess, masks . . . statues, sewing catalogs, [and] pictures."

BIBLIOGRAPHY

Allison, Graham. "Nuclear Terrorism: The Ultimate Preventable Catastrophe." *Carnegie Council* (November 2004). http://www.cceia.org/resources/transcripts/5049.html (accessed March 17, 2010).

Beinart, Peter. "Obama Outsmarts the Terrorists." *The Daily Beast* (February 2, 2005). http://www.thedailybeast.com/blogs-and-stories/2010-02-04/the-dirty-secrit-of-the-terror-war/?cid+bs:featured1 (accessed December 5, 2009).

Belasco, Amy. "Congressional Research Service Report for Congress: The Cost of Iraq, Afghanistan, and Other Global War on Terror Operations Since 9/11." *Congressional Budget Office.* (September 28, 2009). http://www.fas.org/sgp/crs/natsec/RL33110.pdf (accessed November 5, 2009).

Bergen, Peter and Paul Cruickshank. "Is Al Qaida in Pieces?" *The Independent* (June 22, 2005). http://www.independant.co.uk/news/world/asia/special-report-is-al-qaida-in-p.htmls-850606.html (accessed April 20, 2010).

Bergen, Peter. "The Long Hunt for Osama." *The Atlantic* (October 2004). http://theatlantic.com/magazine/archive/2004/10/the-long-hunt-for-osama/3508/ (accessed May 4, 2010).

Bush, George W. *The National Security Strategy of the United States of America.* Washington, D.C.: The White House, September 2002.

———. "President Discusses Global War on Terror" Capital Hilton Hotel, September 5, 2006, http://www.whitehouse/news/releases/2006/09//20060905-4.gov (accessed October 5, 2009).

———. "The National Security Strategy of The United States of America, 2006." http://georgewbush-whitehouse.archives.gov/nsc/nss/2006/ (accessed January 4, 2010).

Carr, David. "The Futility of 'Homeland Defense.'" *The Atlantic* (January 2002). http://www.theatlantic.com/doc/200201/carr (accessed February 23, 2010).

Casey, George W. *2009 Army Posture Statement.* http://www.army.mil/aps/09/2009 _army_posture_statement_web.pdf (accessed March 5, 2010).

Central Intelligence Agency. *World Fact Book.* http://www.cia.gov/library/publications/the-world-factbook/geos/us.html (accessed April 10, 2010).

Department of the Army. *Field Manual 3-24: Counterinsurgency.* Washington, DC: Headquarters Department of the Army, 2006.

Department of Defense. *Joint Publication 1-02: Department of Defense Dictionary of Military and Associated Terms,* (April 12, 2001). http://www.bits.de/NRANEU/others/jp-doctrine/jp1_02(01).pdf (accessed March 5, 2010).

Friedman, Thomas L. *From Beirut to Jerusalem.* New York: Anchor Books, 1990.

———. "Longitudes and Attitudes: Exploring the World After September 11." *Thomas L. Friedman.com* (2002). http://www.thomaslfriedman.com/bookshelf/ longitùdes-and-attitudes/prologue (accessed May 5, 2010).

Frontline Osama bin Laden, "Interview Osama Bin Laden," *Frontline* (May 1998), under "bin Laden Interview," http://www.pbs.org/wgbh/pages/frontline/shows/binladen/who/interview.html (accessed March 16, 2010).

Galula, David. *Counterinsurgency Warfare: Theory and Practice.* St. Petersburg, FL: Hailer Publishing, 2005.

Hoffman, Bruce. *Inside Terrorism.* New York: Columbia University Press, 2006.

————. "The Logic of Suicide Terrorism." *The Atlantic* (June 2003). http://www.theatlantic.com/doc/200306/hoffman (accessed March 17, 2010).

Ibrahim, Raymond. *The Al Qaeda Reader.* New York: Doubleday, 2007.

Imani, Amil. "Jews as Scapegoats," *Jihad Watch.* http://amilimani.com/index.php?option =com_context&task=view&id=175&Itemid=2 (accessed March 2010).

Laipson, Ellen. "While America Slept: Understanding Terrorism and Counterterrorism." *Foreign Affairs*, (January/February 2003). http://www.foreignaffairs.com/articles/58630/ellen-laipson/while-america-slept-understanding-terrorism-and-counterterrorism (accessed March 2, 2010).

Lawrence, Bruce. *Messages To The World: The Statements Of Osama Bin Laden.* New York: Verso Books, 2005.

Lewis, Bernard. *The Middle East and the West.* New York: Harper & Row, 1966.

————. "The Roots of Muslim Rage." *The Atlantic* (September 1990). http://www.theatlantic.com/199009/muslim-rage (accessed February 23, 2010).

————. "What Went Wrong." *The Atlantic* (January 2002). http://www.atlantic/doc/200201/lewis (accessed January 2010).

Lia, Brynjar. "Al-Qaida's Appeal: Understanding its Unique Selling Points." *Perspectives on Terrorism* Vol II, no. 8 (May 2008).

Lipton, Eric, Eric Schmitt, and Mark Mazzetti. "Review of Jet Bomb Plot Shows More Missed Clues." *New York Times* (January 17, 2010). http://www.nytimes.com/2010/01/18/us/18intel.html (accessed April 15, 2010).

Malik, S. K. B. *The Quranic Concept of War.* New Delhi, India: Himalayan Books, 1986.

Meyer, Josh. "Onetime Al Qaeda Loyalists Now Fault It." *Los Angeles Times* (April 24, 2008). http://articles.latimes.com/2008/apr/24/world/fg-qaeda24 (accessed March 27, 2010).

bin Laden, Osama. "Declaration of the World Islamic Front for Jihad Against the Jews and the Crusaders." Translated by *The NEFA Foundation.* http://www.nefafoundation.org/miscellaneous/ FeaturedDocs/nefaubfatwaworldislamicfront.pdf (accessed March 24, 2010).

————. "Statement to the American People." Translated by *The NEFA Foundation.* www.nefafoundation.org miscellaneous/ FeaturedDocs/nefaubfatwaworld islamicfront.pdf (accessed March 24, 2010).

Pape, Robert A. *Dying to Win: The Strategic Logic of Suicide Terrorism.* New York: Random House, 2006.

Patai, Raphael. *The Arab Mind.* New York: Hatherleigh Press, 2002.

Peters, Ralph. "Terrorizing Terrorists." *New York Post* (February 4, 2010). http://www.nypost.com/p/news/opinon/opedcolumnists/terrorizing_terrorists_2DSSsUhLN70IZRRLIK (accessed March 14, 2010).

Qutb, Seyyed. *Milestones.* Damascus: Dar Al-Ilm, 1964.

Raban, Jonathan. "Truly, Madly, Deeply Devout." *The Guardian* (March 2, 2002). http://www.guardian.co.uk/education/2002/mar/02/socialsciences.highereducation (accessed March 17, 2010).

Riedel, Bruce. "The Search for Al Qaeda: Its Leadership, Ideology, and Future." *The Brookings Institution* (March 9, 2010). http://www.brookings.edu/events/2010/ 0309_al_qaeda.aspx (accessed March 10, 2010).

Rumsfeld, Donald. "GWOT Memo." *USA Today* (May 20, 2005). http://www.usatoday.com/ news/washington/executive/rumsfeld-memo.htm (accessed December 15, 2009).

Schanzer, Jonathan. "At War With Whom: A Short History of Radical Islam." *Doublethink* (Spring 2002). http://www.meforum.org/168/at-war-with-whom (accessed April 18, 2010)

Scheuer, Michael. *Marching Toward Hell, America and Islam After Iraq.* New York: Free Press, 2008.

Schwartz-Barcott, T.P. *War, Terror & Peace In The Quran And In Islam.* Carlisle: The Army War College Foundation Press, 2004.

Segeman, Marc. *Understanding Terror Networks.* Philadelphia, PA: University of Pennsylvania Press, 2004.

Smith, J.W. "The Rise and Decline of the Ottoman Empire." *Global Issues* (September 2001). http:// www.globalissues.org/article/247/the -rise-and-decline-of-the-ottoman-empire (accessed February 2010).

Stern, Jessica, cited in *Al Qaeda Now: Understanding Today's Terrorists*, Karen J. Greenberg, Ed., New York: Cambridge University Press, 2005, 36-39.

Stolberg, Sheryl G. and Helene Cooper. "Obama Adds Troops, but Maps Exit Plan," *New York Times* (December 1, 2009). http://www.nytimes.com/2009/12/02/world/asia/02prexy. html?r=1&ref=asia (accessed December 2, 2009).

Sun-Tzu. *The Art of War.* Boulder, CO: Westview Press, 1994.

Tapper, Jake. "Admiral Mullen Rallies U.S. Troops: Slope on This Insurgency Is Going in the Wrong Direction." *Political Punch*, December 11, 2009. http://blogs.abcnews.com/politicalpunch/ 2009/12/adm-mullen-rallies-us-troops-slope-on-this-insurgency-is-going-in-the-wrong-direction.html (accessed April 2010).

Turabian, Kate L. *A Manual for Writers of Research Papers, Theses, and Dissertations,* 7th ed. Chicago: University of Chicago Press, 2007.

United States Department of Defense. *Casualty Update*, http://www.defense.gov/ (accessed April 28, 2010).

Wright, Lawrence. *The Looming Tower: Al-Qaeda and the Road to 9/11.* New York: Alfred A Knopf, 2006.

———. "The Rebellion Within: An Al Qaeda Mastermind Questions Terrorism." *The New Yorker* (June 2, 2008). http://newyorker.com/reporting/2008/06/02/080602fa_fact _wright (accessed May 4, 2010).

Zogby International. "Arab Opinions on President Obama's First 100 Days: A 6 Nation Survey." (May 2004). http://www.aaiusa.org/page/polls/6%20NationPPT%20Finl.pdf (accessed April 4, 2010).

Zuhur, Sherifa. "Precision in the GWOT: Inciting Muslims Through the War of Ideas." (April 2008). http://www.strategicstudiesinstitute.army.mil/ (accessed March 20,. 2010).

9/11 Panel. "Al Qaeda Planned to Hijack 10 Planes." *The 9/11 Commission Report.* (June 16, 2004). http://www.cnn.com/2004/ALLPOLITICS/06/16/ 911.commission/index.html (accessed March 17, 2010).